DSC SPEED READS

PERSONAL DEVELOPMENT

Networking

Debra Allcock Tyler

dsc
directory of social change

Published by the Directory of Social Change (Registered Charity no. 800517 in England and Wales)

Registered address: Directory of Social Change, First floor, 10 Queen Street Place, London, EC4R 1BE

Tel: 020 4526 5995

Visit www.dsc.org.uk to find out more about our books, subscription funding website and training events. You can also sign up for e-newsletters so that you're always the first to hear about what's new.

The publisher welcomes suggestions and comments that will help to inform and improve future versions of this and all of our titles. Please give us your feedback by emailing publications@dsc.org.uk.

It should be understood that this publication is intended for guidance only and is not a substitute for professional advice. No responsibility for loss occasioned as a result of any person acting or refraining from acting can be accepted by the author or publisher.

Print and digital editions first published 2023

ISBN 978 1 78482 110 4 (print edition)
ISBN 978 1 78482 111 1 (digital edition)

British Library Cataloguing in Publication Data
A catalogue record for this book is available from the British Library

Cover and text design by Kate Griffith
Printed and bound in the UK by Martins the Printers, Berwick upon Tweed

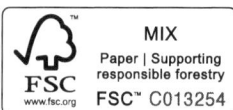

Contents

Introduction

Who will this book help?

This guide is for anyone at any level who works in or volunteers for a charity and wishes to become better at making connections and to amplify their charity's work.

What will it give you?

This book will help you to understand what effective networking is, what to do and not to do, and how to maintain relationships once they are built.

It looks at the differences between in-person and virtual networking, explores the common errors people make when networking and gives tips on how to engage with people you don't know in order to get support for your cause.

Chapter 1

The power of networking

This chapter explains why networking can open doors for your organisation, the common networking mistakes and where you can find networking opportunities.

Why network?

The sole purpose of networking is to create relationships. That is all. And the relationships that you form when networking matter because charities cannot operate in a vacuum. We need supporters, partners, donors and cheerleaders in order to do our work. We need people to care about our charity as much we do and to be ambassadors for our work when we are not there to do it ourselves.

With successful networking you will build strong relationships such that people will advocate for you, both when asked and when unprompted. They can also become a personal advocate for you as an individual – someone you can trust and rely on. They may talk about you and your cause to their contacts, allies and friends. They may lay the ground for you so that you can develop more new relationships by introducing you to others who might be able to help. These relationships may come to nothing; they may produce a meaningful friendship or working partnership; they may result in a donation. Whatever the outcome, building up a bank of friends for your charity is never a bad thing.

However, I have a confession to make. I am a good networker – for the most part – because I know how important it is and have practised hard over time to become effective at it. But, personally, I hate networking with a passion. I can 'perform' in public spaces, I can be gregarious if I know I have to be, but I dread it. The thought of walking into a room full of people I don't know, or who don't know me, or having to connect virtually with someone I've never actually met, fills me with horror. That may be true for many of you too.

The thing is, though, when you work in the voluntary sector, you pretty much have no choice. If you don't introduce your charity, your cause and yourself to others, you limit the possibility of finding new supporters, donors or volunteers. They don't just magically appear. You have to go and look for them.

It is much harder to campaign for change or influence policy and decision makers if you haven't built up relationships or aren't known to those people who have the power to make change. And networking isn't restricted to the trustees, CEOs or people at senior leadership level. Fundraisers, campaigners, front-line workers and volunteers will also often find themselves in situations where they have the opportunity to build relationships that can help further their charity's cause. So, all of us who don't drool with pleasure at the thought of accosting strangers, we just have to suck it up if we care about the work that we do.

The traditional advice around networking (whether that's virtual or in person) and reasons to do it is that you should think about what you and your organisation want to achieve out of a particular networking activity. Typically, that advice consists of being clear about your specific aim. For example:

- To inform someone about your cause.
- To help someone know more about your charity (which may not be the same as learning about your cause).

- To make a connection which may be useful to you in the future.
- To get someone to become a donor, supporter or volunteer.
- To get to know someone because they have connections that they can introduce you to.
- To hear others' challenges and share your own.

These are all valid, but – as I said right at the start – the main purpose is to create relationships. Really powerful networking means you think beyond a short-term ask.

If you start with the aim of achieving something specific from someone through your networking, it will most likely influence how they respond to you in return. No amount of faking it will help you make it – most people recognise when others want something from them. Additionally, sometimes people will make erroneous assumptions about what you want from the interaction. This is common in policy work, where often government or local authorities will quickly assume you will be asking for money when, in fact, you just want to discuss a change in law or policy.

> **Top tip**
>
> Be there when people need you most. Reach out when you see someone at a low point. Offer genuine sympathy and support if someone is suffering a bad day – especially in the media or online.

If you go into a networking opportunity hoping to achieve one clear goal, your thinking is too short-term and too narrow. Suppose you don't achieve your specific aim with that one individual in that single opportunity. There is a danger that you will end up feeling like you have failed and, disheartened, you will miss out on wider and perhaps unexpected opportunities that might have presented themselves to you with this person or other people at the event. Powerful networking involves thinking about what others – not just you – might want or need out of it and focusing on building the relationship over the longer term. It also requires understanding what assumptions others may be making about your intentions so that you can dispel them early. Understanding the 'why' of networking is the first step to doing it successfully.

Case study – The long run

As part of networking many years ago, I formed a good relationship with a then government minister. I maintained the relationship even when he stood down as an MP and moved on to other things that weren't really going to help my organisation.

However, over ten years after I had first met him, he contacted me out of the blue with an opportunity to influence a government policy that he'd been asked to advise on. So thinking long-term and valuing the relationship over what he could do for me immediately actually resulted in a real opportunity for me to influence something very important for the sector.

Mistakes and how to avoid them

While some people find networking a natural skill, many of us don't. We are unsure how to make the first approach, how to create a conversation that feels natural and unforced, and how to follow up appropriately afterwards.

Top tip

Don't seek out the MIPR (Most Important Person in the Room). Treat everyone as important – because they are.

Eleanor Roosevelt reputedly said, 'If you approach every new person you meet in a spirit of adventure, you will find yourself endlessly fascinated by the new channels of thought and experience and personality that you encounter.' But a common mistake folk make is thinking that the individual they need to befriend is the one they assume to be the most important or highest-status person – the Most Important Person in the Room. Someone with a big job title, a big wallet or a big following. It is rarely the case.

I knew a CEO who had the reputation of being the most consummate networker. The problem was that, when you were chatting with him, you could often see him scouring the room in search of someone more important to talk to. Once he'd spotted a more promising prospect, you'd be dumped as he beetled off to talk to the new person. Everyone knew he did it and no one respected him for it, including the Most Important Person in the Room!

Case study – How not to make friends

When I first started as a CEO, I was invited to a reception at the House of Lords. I was chatting to the chair of trustees of my organisation when a well-known CEO of a large and famous charity scuttled over. He didn't know who I was and, instead of introducing himself to me, he completely ignored me and cut across what I was saying to begin talking to my chair. My chair interrupted him to introduce me, 'This is Debra Allcock Tyler.' He briefly paused and somewhat dismissively asked me if I was part of the admin support for the event. My chair then corrected him to say that I was actually their new CEO. His eyes lit up and he began to pay attention to me. Nothing has ever annoyed me more. When he thought I was 'just' admin, he had no interest in me whatsoever. He only cared when he thought I was someone important.

Don't make the mistake of considering front-desk personnel or conference organisers not worthy of your attention. When it comes to networking, *everyone* matters – because everyone can influence others. I was once a junior administrator, and I haven't forgotten those who were dismissive of me then. If I came across them again as a CEO now, I doubt that I would be able to see past how they treated me then. Today's accounts assistant may well be tomorrow's CEO or chair. And not only that – they may also have connections via family, friends or other organisations that they are involved with that you know nothing about. Here's the thing. People will know if they are a 'chore' on your list (so that you can go back to work and say you met them), or if you're just after something and are not particularly interested in them or their work.

If you are at a senior level in an organisation, it is important to keep your feet on the ground. Pay attention to what your teams think of those people and organisations with which you are considering networking. Your staff will give you a wider perspective on the advisability of those associations. If a member of my team thinks the person trying to connect with me is a bit of a twonk, then they will tell me so. And my team's views will influence how willing or to what degree I am likely to engage with them. Always remember that, just as you pay attention to what your colleagues think of others, you can pretty much guarantee that others will pay attention to what their staff, peers and volunteers think too.

If you want to engage with people, you need to start with them: what they want and need – not what you want and need. People respond more to those who appear to be genuinely interested in what they have to say and are keen to give (free!) support. If people sense something comes with a cost, that immediately affects how open they are to you.

> **Where next?**
>
> *How to Win Friends and Influence People* by Dale Carnegie.
>
> Based on courses Carnegie was running on human relations and public speaking, the book was written in 1936, but many of its lessons (not necessarily the language!) remain very relevant today.

Networking opportunities

Essentially, wherever you are coming into contact with others, either physically or virtually, you are presented with a networking opportunity. Often, we don't recognise such situations as networking opportunities, so we fail to make the most of them.

When thinking about networking, many of us imagine being in a group gathering in a room with a glass of something to hand and pinning some poor person down with our eloquent description of our charity or cause. But, in fact, there are so many other 'pinch points' – encounters that can enable you to make the first move and open the space for conversation – where you can begin the process of networking. Opportunities include those before or after you enter the main room where you are all gathering, or at various points of an online event or social media interaction:

- Walking into a venue at the same time as someone
- Getting in the lift
- Collecting a name badge at the front desk
- Getting refreshments
- Finding a seat
- Leaving the event
- Attending a webinar or virtual conference
- Social media that you engage with regularly (and particularly the private chat functions of any platforms)
- Newsletters you receive
- Using the live group chat functions when attending virtual events, webinars or meetings

Overall, the opportunities to network are boundless – the key is to be ready for them, and that is what we explore further in chapter 2.

Chapter 2

Being prepared

This chapter looks at how to be ready for networking.

Do your research

There is no excuse in this day and age for meeting people at planned events, whether physical or virtual, and knowing nothing about them. A five-minute online search will take you to a social media account or a web page where you can learn something about the human being with whom you wish to interact, who they work for, what they and their organisations do and what they care about. If you don't know who is going to be at an event you are attending until it starts, then modern technology makes it easy to do a quick online search in the lobby or the virtual equivalent thereof.

The people who try to network with me and who impress me the most are those who have taken the trouble to find out a bit about me and my organisation. I don't expect them to be experts, but the honest truth is that if someone says, 'I'd like to connect and find out more about what DSC does', I just feel irritated. As do many of my peers. DSC's website tells you what we do – it links to our social media accounts, including mine, so it is really easy to look us up. If, however, they say, 'I see from your website and social media that you do a lot of work on governance and I'd like to get your advice', that is much more appealing to me. They've indicated they know something about what we do and they've asked for my help rather than making me feel that they want

> **Top tip**
> Think about your timing. Consider in which moments the person may be available or more receptive to you.

to sell me something. Demonstrating some understanding of the person, their work and their organisation goes a long way to beginning a relationship.

You will be more effective at creating relationships if you make others feel that they are likely to gain something from meeting you rather than that you are after something from them. Before you attend the event, try to imagine yourself in the shoes of those you will be networking with: what they might want from you and how your conversation might run. Anticipating those things shows that you are thoughtful and well prepared.

How you appear

It's important to think in advance about the image you will be presenting. If you look as if you haven't bothered with your appearance, folk will subconsciously judge you on it. Not fair? Sure. But the reality? Absolutely! Whether you like it or not, in order to build a relationship with people, you will need to be thinking about how you appear, behave and overall present yourself. Crucially, at those 'pinch points' where you're engaging people for the first time and networking with complete strangers, it is likely to influence how they see you and how they subconsciously 'file' you in their head. And this is as much true for how you appear online as how you appear in person.

What you wear

If you happen to work from home at least some of the time, you may feel that it doesn't matter if you're in a slightly crumpled T-shirt with your favourite band on it. But you can still be seen – even if it's just the shoulders up. Remember that your clothes are a tool that you use depending on the environment in which you are operating. You wouldn't wear a bikini to a funeral or a suit to the beach. A work environment is just another setting. This is not about wearing formal suits all the time – it's about, at the very least, not dressing in a way that leads people to make the sorts of judgement about you that you don't want. Ask yourself what image you want to leave in people's minds and then dress accordingly. My rule of thumb is: don't wear things that get in the way or distract from your message.

It is, however, worth trying to wear or accessorize with something distinctive. I have a fantastic pair of silver cowboy boots which do two things when I wear them: they're definitely a conversation starter, as they're so eye-catching, and they help people to remember me. Similarly, I tend to wear colourful scarves when appearing online. At the very least, memorable outfit details can be a starting point for someone to open a conversation with you. And it works the other way round too: approaching someone with 'Great tie!' or 'Love your shoes' invariably goes down well.

Case study – Wear your personality

I know a book editor who wears a tie adorned with classic mid-20th century book covers. The great thing about it for networking is that the visual flag immediately identifies their line of work, and brief questioning quickly pinpoints their job role. So it is both a simple shortcut to saying what they do and a great starting point for conversation; it's distinctive and everyone has an opinion on which books they recognise or particularly like.

How you write

Your written communication reflects on your image as much as your appearance does. Think in advance about how you craft all written communications. Don't make the mistake of thinking that just because you're in an online chat, you can ignore the basic rules of grammar and punctuation. While some folk won't care if you haven't spelt something correctly, there will inevitably be those who do. In my experience, it's always better to assume that people notice these things and that it influences how they see you. Don't lose a great opportunity because you carelessly put an apostrophe in the wrong place or used outdated language. And, unless you're already in a close relationship with someone and it is mutually accepted, avoid 'text speak'. Using things like 'Gr8, cu @8!' rarely comes across as efficient and is more likely to confuse. Besides, the person may feel you don't consider them worthy of your time if you can't spare a few seconds to type a handful of extra characters.

Don't start emails or chats with just someone's name – that can come across as rude or cold. Use a greeting – 'Hi Debra' is better than just 'Debra'. And be sure you get their name right! People's names really matter. In any room with a buzz of conversation, the word that will always prick people's attention is their own name. Don't call people by their 'familiar' names unless they invite you to. Find out how people want to be called (or how they introduce themselves) and use that. If I am Debra on LinkedIn or introduce myself as such, don't refer to me as Debbie or Debs, for example. If I sign off with Debs, then I am implicitly giving you permission to refer to me that way.

Equally, think about your sign-offs. Consider how something that you're quite used to may be interpreted by a person with different habits. For example, 'Regards' can be perceived as not particularly warm. (In fact, whenever I receive it from someone, I often suspect they're a bit cross!) Tone often gets completely lost in writing. Signing off with a genuine 'Looking forward to working with you' or 'Really glad to have connected' will make it clearer how you feel than just 'Kind regards' – however kind they are! Think about how you can end your communication with language that conveys warmth.

How you engage

When preparing for networking engagements, think of these three key things:

1. How are you going to make sure that you are able to contact someone after the event?

With in-person networking, you may exchange business cards. Do you have any and are they up to date? Do you know how you can quickly exchange

> **Top tip**
>
> LinkedIn has a QR code facility that enables you to share your details via a single click.
>
> *www.linkedin.com/help/li nkedin/answer/a525286/ using-a-linkedin-qr-code- to-connect-with- members?*

contact details via Bluetooth? With virtual networking, have you got all your details to hand to quickly cut and paste them into the chat function? Do you know how to message people directly on a virtual conference/webinar/call and on social media? Are you familiar with how the different platforms work?

2. Is there any particular point that you want your new contact to take away from their interaction with you?

Think about one (and only one!) key thing that you want people to remember after they interact with you, so that when you do contact them, they can more easily recall it. It might be the fact that your organisation is the biggest charity in the region, or that you have a very strong relationship with your local councillor, or that your charity has won an award. Think about the ways in which you might weave that information into your conversations.

3. How do you want them to remember you?

Maya Angelou famously said that people forget what you said, forget what you did but never forget how you made them feel. How do you want others to feel after their interaction with you? Do you want them to feel inspired? Think about the message you could share and the energy you'll need to bring to create that feeling. Do you want them to feel admired by you? How will you show your admiration so it feels genuine?

Being prepared is crucial in networking. It will both ease some of that 'performance' anxiety and ensure that you make the most out of every networking opportunity – however unexpected.

Chapter 3

In-person networking

This chapter looks at the value of networking face to face and offers some top tips for doing it successfully.

The value of in-person networking

I have become much more skilled at virtual networking through necessity since the COVID-19 pandemic, and virtual networking definitely saves time and resources. But I feel that in-person connections are probably the most effective and powerful if you can find opportunities to engage in them.

From a psychological perspective, when you are in the same space as someone, you can pick up on things that are absent from a screen. You can sense how engaged they are with you by picking up on subtle body language, such as the way they move their feet or make eye contact. Based on these cues, you can adjust where the conversation is going and your responses accordingly.

You can also carry out common courtesies, such as offering to get the person a drink or telling them where the loos are. These small touches that show you are interested in their comfort are nice to receive and build a sense of liking and trust. These things are harder to do virtually (see chapter 4 for more on virtual networking).

Another benefit of in-person networking is the ability to connect physically through a handshake or a hug (where appropriate and with permission, obviously!). I've noticed that, since the pandemic, people are less likely to want to touch each other. I understand why but still think this is a pity. Physical touch creates a human connection on a subconscious level and makes folk more inclined to be open to each other. Do offer to shake hands where you feel it's appropriate.

Network from the outset

Remember that networking opportunities start from the minute you enter the building. There's a good chance that someone is queuing for their badge at the same time as you or is equally confused about the floor map. That's a good starting point – you've already got something in common.

> **Top tip**
> Folks can quickly forget your name and be too embarrassed to ask again. Wear a clearly placed badge – or bring your own professional one if you can.

Despite how confident people may appear on the outside, many feel nervous about going into unfamiliar surroundings and meeting others for the first time. Some simple rules to break the ice are:

- Start by acknowledging that you're attending the same event. Such as, 'Oh, are you here for the so and so event? Me too.'

- Introduce yourself with your full name, your organisation and what you do there. So, 'My name is Debra Allcock Tyler, CEO of DSC, lovely to meet you.'

- Don't shy away from obvious questions, e.g. 'Have you been to one of these things before?' It's a gentle introduction without being too pushy.

- Listen to what they say. Don't start by banging on about yourself – although if you feel nervous about networking events, it does no harm to admit it. Making yourself vulnerable helps other people to feel reassured, and there's a good chance they feel the same. Saying 'I always feel a bit nervous at these events' shows you're human and offers the opportunity to engage with you by either sharing their own vulnerability or offering reassurance.

18

- Do *not* dump the person the minute you get into the room/event. But do allow them to move away from you if they want to.

Importantly, think about the quality of the questions you are asking. It can be frustrating when someone you don't know well, or indeed at all, asks what challenges you are facing or 'what's going on in your organisation?'. Keep it simple by asking people why they're at the event or what their organisation does (unless you're quick or lucky enough to land on someone you've researched in advance, in which case you can refer to something their organisation is involved in or ask them how long they've been there).

And remember, it's perfectly normal to engage in small talk – refer to the weather, ask where they have travelled from or comment on public transport. You don't need to charge straight in with interrogating them about their thoughts on the political environment! Start with what feels natural.

In the room

At breaks, receptions, informal gatherings

It's quite intimidating to be in any gathering if you don't know anyone, so it's fine to look for someone you do know first. If there's a familiar face, go over to them and say hi. Even if they are talking to someone else, you can join the group. You don't need to cut in and say anything. The person you know will likely invite you to join in. And if they don't, don't hang around like a spare part – quietly retreat if you feel uncomfortable or that you're invading their space.

When someone introduces you, repeat what they have said with more information. If they say 'This is Debra', offer to shake hands with others in the group and add some further detail. For example, 'Hi, I'm Debra Allcock Tyler, CEO of DSC, nice to meet you.' And where someone invites you to a conversation without any introduction, make sure you still begin by introducing yourself. Too often we're embarrassed to introduce ourselves – but it's key to successful networking. What is the point of saying something

19

searingly interesting if no one knows who you are and won't remember you afterwards?

Top tip

If you follow somebody on social media, say so! It shows that you're interested in someone in their public space.

If the other people don't offer their name, ask. You can say, 'I'm so sorry, I didn't catch your name.' If you recognise them but haven't met them, acknowledge it with something like, 'Ah, you're the CEO of Blingdy Charity, aren't you?' or whatever is appropriate.

Lots of folk introduce themselves to me by telling me they follow me on social media, which embarrasses and pleases me in equal measure. But it always makes me want to talk to them. It's even more impressive if you say which particular post or article you found inspiring or why it was relevant to your own organisation.

One of the best things you can do at these sorts of occasions is to introduce folk to each other. If you see someone hovering around your group or standing alone, invite them in (even if you don't know them). Start by introducing yourself and asking them who they are, and then invite others to introduce themselves too. Think of yourself as a kind of 'host' at a party where you want people to mix and get to know each other. Facilitating opportunities for others to connect is a great way to get yourself noticed. People remember those who helped them to feel comfortable and meet others. Be generous – share your friends and welcome strangers.

Sitting down

I have some very simple rules for when you are attending a conference or a meeting. Do not sit down without properly introducing yourself to those you're sat next to (so just a 'hello' won't do!). I will keep repeating this – always, always give your name and organisation (and job title if appropriate). That will help folk to reciprocate and tell you who they are. It also opens the opportunity for a conversation while you're waiting for the event or session to start.

Definitely don't whisper asides to others during the session or speech (most people – not least the person presenting – find that irritating) but do ask them at a natural break what they think about what they've heard. Don't start with what *you* think. For starters, you might put them off sharing their opinion if it's different. Plus, you already know what *you* think! Give yourself the opportunity to hear a different perspective.

> **Top tip**
> Sit at the front or as near to the front as possible, so you can be seen by the speakers as well as the people behind you.

And whatever you do, don't be snarky about the speaker or the content – even if your fellow attendee agrees, it's not a good look. Discuss the session calmly without personalising criticism. To deride or mock is a sure way to leave a poor impression about how you engage. People will be left wondering what you say about them when they're not there!

If you see something differently to someone you're interacting with, don't say 'I disagree' or 'You're wrong', say 'That's interesting. I see it differently' and explain why. People don't like to be made to feel wrong and it is more likely to cement their original view – but they're often open to a different perspective if that is how you've framed it.

Do	Don't
Introduce yourself in full every time you meet someone new.	Assume people know who you are or that they don't want to talk.
Introduce folk to each other.	Assume everyone knows everyone.
Invite people into your group even if you don't know them.	Ignore those who are standing alone.
Ask questions.	Talk about yourself or your organisation to the exclusion of others.
Use your body language to show you're interested.	Look around for other, more important people.

The key thing to note is that you want to be memorable – that will make it easier to follow up later.

Chapter 4

Virtual networking

This chapter focuses on the challenges of networking online.

How virtual networking has changed the game

When I first joined the voluntary sector, networking tended to be face to face: at conferences, fundraising events, meetings or specially organised networking events. The world has changed a great deal since then – partly because of the COVID-19 pandemic and partly because of the convenience of technology – and now virtual networking is much more common. The ease of meeting a vast range of people (in terms of both roles and geographic spread) in the comfort of your own office or home and often easily squeezed in between other work is irresistible.

There are now myriad ways in which you can meet and network with others in the virtual world, including:

- online meetings;
- webinars;
- conference calls;
- social media platforms.

All of these give you so many different virtual opportunities to interact – and so many ways you can get it right or get it wrong.

Why we so often get it wrong

I'm not convinced that many of us understood how to translate face-to-face behaviours into the virtual world. And it matters because online interaction is often our first vital point of contact with people and the first chance to make a good impression.

The reason we so often get virtual interactions horribly wrong is partly because we don't prepare ourselves for online events as thoroughly as we might do for in-person events (see chapter 2). Also, our behaviours change when we are in front of a screen rather than in front of or beside a person in real life. Because we don't always see a person's face when we connect online, we may introduce ourselves in a way that would mortify us if we did it face to face!

We tend to communicate electronically in a way that forgets we are all human beings. For example, we set aside any niceties, such as introducing ourselves warmly; we can fall into the trap of immediately going after what we want from the event or session when we would never do that in person; we give information straight away without engaging; and we make assumptions about how people want to be addressed. Behaving with in-person courtesy in the virtual environment and following online behaviour protocols really help to make networking opportunities a better experience for all involved.

> **Where next?**
> Read up on some suggested Zoom protocols:
>
> *www.technology.pitt.edu/ blog/zoom-tips*

Your use of words

Some people engage online by using off-putting business speak. You can sense that someone is doing a mass marketing thing when they say something like 'I'm reaching out to you' (bleuch) or 'I'm wanting to connect'. It sounds like they're not thinking about how to engage with you as an individual.

Don't use language in the virtual world that you wouldn't use in the physical world. It feels unnatural and may jar. Be yourself.

Things *not* to say when connecting:

- I came across your profile and thought you looked interesting (can appear patronising)
- I just wanted to check if this might be of interest (can sound as if you're selling something)
- I don't want to pester you but... (yes you do)
- I'd love to learn a bit more about you (nosy)
- I know I've messaged you a few times but ...(this one is particularly annoying – if I didn't respond the first time, I'm probably not interested!)
- I think we have a lot in common (based on what?)

Better things to say:

- My name is X and I do Y. I've been looking at the work that you do and I'd like to talk about how I can support it/ask for your advice. If you're not the right person, would you mind letting me know who the best person is?
- I'm so sorry to contact you again – it's possible that you didn't see my first message or didn't have time to get back to me. I promise I won't get in touch again if you did see it and are not interested.

And then leave them alone!

Networking at online events

Webinars and similar online sessions are among the most valuable opportunities for networking. They're not just about learning whatever the topic is; they also automatically give you an opportunity to meet and engage with others. There are many ways to connect with others. You can message individuals using the chat facility, use emojis to show that you like something they've said or show approval by your facial expression. These are useful shortcuts to getting yourself noticed in online settings and sparking off an interaction with someone you want to connect with.

Being visible in the event

First, when you sign in to the event, ensure that you are 'labelled' appropriately. Don't just put your first name or the name of your charity. Just as with in-person introductions, make sure your full name, job title and charity name is clear. It's a good practice to introduce yourself in the chat immediately when you join (e.g. 'Morning all. I'm Debra Allcock Tyler, CEO of DSC. Really looking forward to the session.'). Other will see you've done that and it will encourage them to engage as well.

Top tip
Don't multi-task. It's pretty obvious when someone is checking their emails instead of listening.

There are many reasons why you might prefer to switch your camera off; however, if your goal is to make a connection with people online, one of the most important pieces of advice I can give you is to keep your camera on in a virtual session – even if you're one of hundreds. We rarely remember those we can't see, so being seen is often the start of networking. And if you feel comfortable doing so, leave your camera on as often as you can. I always think that having your camera off is the equivalent of sitting in a conference room with your back to other people and a paper bag over your head. And others might wonder if you have joined the event but are actually paying no attention and doing something else entirely.

People respond to and engage best with faces (and especially with animated facial expressions!). Bear in mind that online you have to exaggerate facial expressions and body language slightly, so that you can be seen and your opinion is obvious. Nod vigorously, smile broadly, clap your hands in front of your face so people can see you're applauding what has been said, show noticeable thumbs-up – it sends a clear message even if people can't hear you.

Also think about how you could use a virtual background to create a talking point or memorable impression – an image of your charity or the people you serve, for example.

Getting known at the event

Being seen at an online event is the first but not the only step. And, for many of us, engaging someone directly can feel a little bit less scary online. Messaging someone you don't know in the event chat function can feel less intimidating than approaching them in person. So make good use of it. To start making specific connections at an online event:

- Comment on what you're hearing in the chat. But do so positively or with a question. Remember that snide criticism of what a speaker is saying will not make a good impression.

- Make good use of emojis. The thumbs-up, clap, celebration and other emojis show that you are engaged and paying attention. That gives an impression of someone interested and interesting. Never leave a webinar without having left an emoji!

- Try to ask questions verbally rather than via the chat function if you can. Raise both your virtual and your physical hand to indicate that you want to say something. Questions asked in chats can get missed and people don't necessarily notice who is asking the question. Questions asked in person mean that you are highlighted on the screen, and people can hear and see you – and therefore are likely to remember you.

- If you are going to directly message someone at the event out of the blue, try to find some common ground – do your charities have common causes, for example? Don't say, 'I'd like to find out more about what you do.' Show you've done your homework.

- When messaging directly, start with something positive: 'I really liked what you just said about X' or 'I'm so impressed with the work you're doing on Y.'

- As the event is coming to an end, use the public chat to offer thanks and praise – and if you thought it was rubbish, don't say anything. I'll repeat: public criticism in this situation does not reflect well on you. If you embarrass the organiser or the other attendees, they won't want to engage with you in the future. Even if you don't connect with anyone this time, you may want to do so at some point in the future.

Networking on social media

Social media is a handy way to make that initial contact with someone, especially where you're unlikely to cross paths with them otherwise. More importantly, the same social media channels are great for staying in touch later (more on that on page 31). It can also be powerful to share things that are challenging or personal to you, so others can see that you face similar issues to them. However, be careful how much of yourself you show in the virtual world. It's important to be authentic, so don't fake a persona that you can't sustain in real life. And at all costs avoid personal criticisms of individuals online – including politicians. It's OK to attack an idea or a policy, and sometimes an institution, but always avoid personal attacks.

Case study – Arthur

There is a simple rule I follow for my social media pages: one-third of it is professional content about my work/charity; one-third is commentary about wider society/politics; and one-third is something personal.

My followers and engagement shot through the roof when I started sharing stories about my daily struggles with the love of my life – my beastly basset Arthur. People click to read about Arthur and end up following me or engaging in the other issues I care about or the work we are doing at DSC.

Find that personal thing about you which you are willing to share and which will help people to find a connection with you – then share it regularly.

Tip	Note
Avoid asking people to be friends on Facebook or similar private friendship sites.	Unless it's an organisation's page – most people won't want their professional network to see personal family posts!
Ask to connect on LinkedIn.	But always send an accompanying message, for example 'I saw you speak at X event' or 'I'm interested in your work in so and so'.
Follow people on social media platforms they are using.	Always send a message that you're connecting so that they have more detail than just your name appearing in the request to connect.
Do engage on social media.	Don't just say, 'I don't do social media.' The reality is that most people do – and certainly younger people, who are your supporters, workers and funders of the future.
Like *and* share.	When you share something someone has posted, it makes them pay attention to you.

Virtual networking has many benefits, not least in that it makes connecting with others a bit less intimidating for those who are not natural networkers. However, just because you're not networking in person, it doesn't mean you can ignore the usual rules around interacting with people. There's still a human being behind that screen!

Chapter 5

Following up

This chapter suggests how to pursue your new connections after you have made the initial contact.

So you've met – now what?

It is vital that you follow up on the initial contacts you have made during an event or another interaction. That doesn't have to be complicated, nor do you have to craft an ask in the first instance. An email, a direct online message or a social media post to say that you enjoyed meeting them, sharing a breakout space with them or hearing what they had to say and asking if they're happy to stay in touch is perfectly sufficient. This way you strengthen that initial link and don't put them off by making them think you're after something. Then, later, if you do think of ways in which you want to collaborate and work with them, the message won't come out of the blue.

Making friends

With follow-up, you are trying to cement the relationship. Think about how you make friends in your personal life. It's rare that you start by asking for something – you tend to offer something first. For example, if you were trying to make friends with the other parents on the school run, you might say things like, 'A group of us meet Fridays for coffee after drop-off, fancy joining us?' or 'Did you know that the PTA has this great recycling school uniform initiative.

Would you like me to message you the date for the next collection and put you in touch with the organiser?'

And, of course, the reverse is also true. If you were the newbie at the school run and wanted to make acquaintances, you might ask about pick-up times or how you might get to know people and if they could help.

That same approach also works in networking, both physical and virtual. You can send a link to a report or book that you think they might find interesting, or share a group that you think they might like to join or find valuable. And, most importantly, introduce them to other people in your network who you think might be useful to them. Share your friends (although always ask permission of the person whose details you are sharing first).

Case study – how not to share friends

I remember once a person I'd met at a networking event emailed me and copied in someone I'd never heard of, saying that we should get to know each other. It made me really not want to. It put me on the spot and I had to find the time to reply and engage, as I didn't want to be rude. And the link wasn't useful. Someone wanted to sell me something. It really put me off the person who had made the connection. If they had asked me first, I would have had the chance to say 'yes, of course' and would have welcomed the introduction, or I could I have said that I'm not the right person and pointed them somewhere else.

If you are asked to meet someone virtually or be introduced via email, try to start with a yes or at least suggest who might be a better person. When you just say no, you put the person asking in a difficult position. They're likely to have promised that someone that they'll try to introduce you, and your refusal to meet will leave a lasting impression with the introducer.

Using social media to stay in touch

Most of us use social media in various forms as a good way to stay in touch. And a really great way to gain a fan is to post something publicly acknowledging that person, their charity or their work. It needs to be genuine, obviously. Seeing someone share something good about you or your work in public really warms people's hearts and makes them want to reciprocate. Be generous and public in your praise.

Never offer negative or critical feedback to someone via social media. It gets people's hackles up. In fact, don't offer specific feedback at all unless you're asked for it. Remember that constructive criticism rarely lands constructively. What you think of as constructive may not feel that way to the recipient. If you don't know the person and you haven't been asked, don't take the risk of offending or annoying – especially in a public space such as social media. If sharing the criticisms is that important to you, take the time and trouble to contact someone directly.

Get into the habit of liking or sharing others' social media posts that you find interesting or engaging. Comment positively if they've said or shared something that you think is interesting or helpful. Although a like is always welcome, there's nothing quite as powerful as a share, which tells the person that you took the time to show their stuff to someone else – so you must value it.

Final words

- Don't allow your nervousness to get in the way of making friends. It's only the first step that's scary! After you've said 'hello', everything becomes easier.
- Remember that you can help yourself by taking care of the details such as your personal appearance and how you communicate in writing and virtually.

- Don't just follow someone – make sure you are actively engaging with them, especially if it's someone you want to build a relationship with.

- Think long term – someone who can't help you now might turn out to be super helpful in years to come.

- Don't be intimidated or swayed by job titles or perceived status. We're all just human beings trying to navigate our way through life.

- You're just making friends. You know how to do that.

Good luck!